Tell Tales

A Book on how to 'Tell Tales'

To Sarah,
with love
Julie
xx

Julie Pryke

**Ideas for Parents, Grandparents,
Teachers, Play-workers
and other storytellers.**

**Includes, as examples, a range of stories
for children aged up to 9 years...**

Illustrations: Joanne Tordoff

Tell Tales

First published 2015 by Beaten Track Publishing
Copyright © 2015 Julie Pryke

A CIP catalogue record for this book
is available from the British Library.

ISBN: 978 1 910635 34 6

Illustrations by Joanne Tordoff

Beaten Track Publishing,
Burscough. Lancashire.
www.beatentrackpublishing.com

Tell Tales Table of Contents

1) Tell Tales – Introduction

This book is for everyone who is interested in reading to children, or making up stories for children to enjoy. Interested? Then, sit back, relax and let me tell you a short tale – of why and how I got involved in storytelling. Then we'll move on to how you might do so too! I'll give you some examples and ideas how to get started. Go on, you know you want to!

Whilst I read a lot to my own children, I really started telling stories, in a regular way, following the birth of my first grandchild, Thomas, in 2005. He lives in Germany with his English dad and German mum. I don't have the immediate closeness of seeing him or his sister Finnja (2008) as often as I would like, so, I tell them stories, on request, almost any time when I am with them, and also when I am speaking to them over the Internet, using a webcam, or on the phone.

As a great believer in stories and storybooks as part of developing a child's love for reading and thirst for knowledge, I soon began making up very short stories for Thomas, using stories I remembered from my own childhood to provide a model for me to work from. Imagine my delight when at three years old he told me his first story back; something on the lines of: *'There was a dog called Peter, and he went to the shop, and he got a bone out of a bag, and he went home.'* Grins of pride and delight on all sides!

Since then I have used every opportunity to develop stories for both of them. Also, my new grandson, Kian (2013, England) already has a few stories, one of which I've included in this collection. But you don't have to be a grandparent to use this book; just someone who is looking forward to developing a healthy, positive relationship with children they know: family, friends, work-related, face-to-face or at a distance.

So, why am I telling you this? Well this book is designed encourage you to move on from just *reading* stories to children and to help you develop your storytelling skills, whether or not you have any experience already. It is NOT saying 'Do it this way!' but is intended to offer a few suggestions to help you along the way. It also includes a few stories and story-games to start you off, if you do not feel confident enough to tell your own just yet. They start as very simple ones for the younger age group and gradually develop to an example suitable for someone around eight or nine years of age, but reflect the skills development of the storyteller (me/you) at the same time.

It may be that you are feeling a bit uneasy at the idea of telling stories to your children; you may think the task is a bit daunting, or that you are not the right person to do this. You may put off attempting to do so because you feel you don't have the skills and very often because you feel 'I haven't got time!'

Or, as a male reader, there may be a gender issue for you; possibly the person who told you stories was a woman: your mother, grandmother, auntie or first teacher. As a result you may unconsciously feel that 'that's what women do', or 'it's more natural for their mum to tell them', or even 'people wouldn't like it if I started telling them stories'. None of these statements are true, although whoever is doing more of the day-to-day caring has more opportunities to develop their skills in this direction (though they may be a bit more tired!). I do hope you do not feel like this, or that you will reconsider your ideas once you've had a little help from this book. You and your listeners will get such pleasure out of this shared activity that it is well worth trying.

Telling stories and reading/being read to are important to me, as they offer so much to the listener/reader by maybe awakening an interest in a new area, or offering solutions to problems, but also because, if they are spoken out loud, they become a warm, shared, comforting experience – with an adult on-hand to take away the fright from a scary situation – even if they created it in the first place! They provide a reference point for future shared conversations and experiences. It is a fun experience, a memorable one and one worth pursuing.

I feel, that everyone has the capacity to tell stories; it may be completely outside your current experience but so was walking, swimming, driving, writing, cooking, at some time in your life. It is practice that makes a good story teller, so look at the 30-second stories and start small. Can you remember something you or a family member did which still makes you chuckle? Tell this as a story and you are on your way! Look at the stories in the book: how would you tell them if the adult character was you, a dad, a grandad, an auntie, or a family friend? What special characteristics and experience would you bring to the stories? Would they be more adventurous, more factual, or funnier? Do what feels best for you!

For me, the device of personalising the stories with the names of my grandchildren, plus including a couple of magic animals (and Nana), has been very useful in helping me imagine situations and outcomes for the stories for the children when they were younger; once you begin telling your own tales try and find a device which will work equally well for you. Perhaps their names, perhaps animal-centred stories, perhaps music or poetry based, or including jokes that they will enjoy. Of course, you are welcome to use the stories in the book and change the names to those of your children – but please do remember that this does not mean that you wrote them, just that they helped you along the way!

And so, we begin! There'll be lots of examples along the way and a chance for you to start practising at the end of most sections or at the end of a chapter. They will give you a chance to start developing or increasing your skills. Just look out for the sections called **'Over to you'**!

2) Developing Characters and Situations

Character Development

One of the most important aspects of storytelling is the development of characters who will be believable for young children and with whom they can associate. In my case, for the most part, I have taken the easy way out, using the children themselves as the main characters. If you decide to use this trick then you do get instant attention from the children as they wonder what on earth they are going to do next. At age three, my granddaughter asked her father, *"Papa, do I really have magic shoes?"* his reply being, *"Yes, you do in Nana's story...but not in real life!"* My grandson, her older brother, loved the idea of racing cars along streets he knows – against fictional characters, usually Super Mario and the others from the cartoon games series!

But as a few more regular characters are needed to make the stories come to life, I took the opportunity to jump into the stories myself; I wanted to have some of the fun too! I wanted the character to be able to make things happen, so I gave myself a few minor magic powers (and the ability to put situations right) and a couple of small wooden ornaments with the names of my real pets – Wanda the cat and Suzi the dog – to do the ridiculous or truly magical things on my behalf.

I decided to describe myself as follows:

> Nana isn't a witch; she just has a little bit of magic at the end of her fingertips, as most nanas do!

I also decided that Wanda was brighter, but more easily scared than Suzi, and that Suzi was excitable – a bit muddle-headed but very happy. A bit like their real life counterparts! Then I just added other characters as needed – friends, toy animals, fairies – whoever happened to pop into my head at the time.

I'm sure you can already begin to think of characters that you might develop through your own stories. If you have used the children listening as characters, think about including yourself, if you think the plot needs an adult they can rely on! Please don't worry about introducing yourself in this way; after all, you are talking to the child(ren) as you are trying to develop the story, and so who better to take a place in it also.

You can also use other family members and friends to help you think of characters; you may not want to use their actual names but they may have characteristics that you could use and which the children will be familiar with. The range of people is endless: Mum, Dad, sister, brother, auntie, uncle, cousin, grandparents. Plus children's friends, teachers, Mum and Dad's friends, neighbours and so on.

Look also at the characteristics and abilities of the child(ren), both physical and mental, and those of others they know, and offer representative characters who take a full part in the stories. If you haven't used the listeners as characters, they will still need to have characters they can relate to in order to get swept along with the story.

Over to you:

Get yourself a notebook or some paper and a pen, pencil, pencil sharpener and rubber. You will probably find that you prefer to write with a pen or with a pencil, and will stick to that whenever you start writing – or you could use a keyboard/tablet/phone, of course, but the pen or pencil feel more satisfactory to me at this stage, partly because it feels more permanent and somehow stimulates my thinking.

Write down your first thoughts for each of these questions. But don't worry about them if you can't yet.

- Who are you writing the story for?

- What kind of child(ren) are they? What are their main characteristics – shy, noisy, enthusiastic or other?

- What kind of stories do they already enjoy?

- Do you want to use their names or other ones as characters?

- What other characters do you need?

- What do you want to do with the story? Challenge them, help them think things out, or reassure them in some way? Or just entertain them and make them feel happy?

Nursery workers, teachers and others working with a group

- Think about the children you work with – what are their names, characters, quirks? How can these be incorporated in your story? Do they need to be?

- Would you just involve one child you work with (under their real name or a pseudonym) or more? Why?

- How can the children contribute towards the story?

Situation and Location Development

These often depend on where I am at the time. If I'm walking along in the park I may describe the characters as being there, or in the woods, then add a squirrel, a pond, and/or something a bit more unexpected, like a magic castle or a piano. If I'm going to the shops with my grandchildren, then I look around at people, in shop windows, at traffic and so on; or I might relate ideas to their school or holiday activities. But I find, and I suspect a lot of people do, that quite often the story takes on a life of its own and I am rapidly having to try and think myself out of situations I didn't intend to get us into. What panic! What fun!

The age, understanding and experience of the individual child plays a large part in how the situations change and grow and you need to develop a sensitivity towards the child before you can truly include them in stories which involve characters that they associate with. Use your own experiences as a child too!

Keep telling the tale and don't be afraid; your stories don't have to be perfect. Remember you've got a very special audience who really appreciate you just talking to them, and the bonus is, they may ask questions, add ideas, or want you to explain something, but they don't have any literary criticism skills; they just love what you are doing! Thanks to my eldest son for pointing this out.

Finally, keep reading, listening to, and watching children's stories and films; there is such a wealth of stories at the moment, and so many talented authors, that time and again you will learn tips about this art from them. They usually start off with a fairly **safe situation** for the characters, an ordinary world – then **someone appears** or **something happens** to provide a **threat, danger or conflict** to be resolved; sometimes the character tries to **avoid becoming involved,** sometimes they meet a **friend or guide** who helps them think the problem though – then along comes the **solution**, whether expected or a complete surprise! The solution may well be a surprise to you too – as often you are just thinking on your feet and only half an idea ahead of the listener to the story. But it does work out! Don't worry! Try thinking about a familiar plot – would you have solved the problem in the same way? Can you develop a different solution?

Told-aloud stories should have plenty of conversation in them, or thinking out loud by the characters, to tell us, **the readers/listeners**, what is going on. Then make sure your idea is pitched at the right level and not boring, repetitive or stilted, and there you have an excellent formula for writing stories. Start reading and listening and you will soon spot the pattern.

Now, let's move on to telling the stories.

Here is a quick one about a father and his two children, with pointers to help you see how I build things up:

Helen, Bobby and Dad

(I just thought of three names)

Helen and Bobby are twins, they are six years old.
(I don't know any twins and I'm not sure yet what will happen.)

One day, whilst Mum was working, they went with Dad for a walk in the park.
(Familiar setting)

There was a big lake in the park with boats on it, and lots of swans and ducks to feed.
(Potential for incident)

Bobby and Helen asked Dad if they could go for a ride in a rowing boat and he said, "Yes."
(More potential)

Dad started rowing and Helen got a bag of stale bread out of her pocket so that they could feed the birds.
(Danger coming)

A big swan came up and tried to grab the bag from her.
(Oh no!)

Bobby stood up to stop it, but he tripped up and fell over the side of the boat with a big *splash* and an even bigger scream (*jokey, it's going to be OK, voice*) into the water!

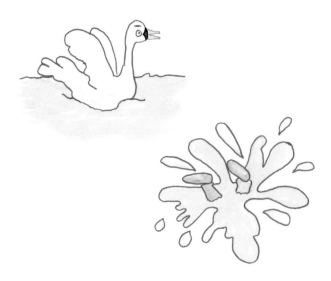

He could swim a bit but was upset and surprised.
(*It's happened!*)

Helen and Dad both shouted, "Dad's coming!" and, "It's OK, I'm here."
(*The rescue started*)

Helen grasped the oars as Dad reached out as quickly as he could and grabbed the back of Bobby's trousers and pulled him back in the boat.
(*Hurray!*)

Dad asked Helen to keep the boat steady with the oars whilst he made sure Bobby was OK.
(*Helen doing something helpful*)

He took his coat off and put it round Bobby to get him warm again and gave him a big hug. He told Bobby how good it was that he'd been able to swim.
(*Praise for Bobby, not a telling-off*)

A man from the boathouse rowed up with a blanket for Bobby and checked that they were all OK.
(*Reassurance*)

He fastened a rope onto the boat and towed them back to the boathouse.
(*Outside help – also reassuring*)

The man let them sit by his warm fire whilst he made them all a hot drink and gave them some biscuits to eat.

(*Comforting*)

Then they thanked him and went home.

(*Happy ending*)

(Only 312 words, excluding my comments)

~~~~~~~~~~

It could just as easily have been Helen who fell in and Bobby who helped Dad; I didn't know which one it would be until I had written it, and it didn't matter which. I hope this helps you to get started! You can choose who to involve and in what way – and you can take into account different factors which might help you decide.

For example, one child might be very shy and would get a boost from being a 'hero' or a sensible person in the story; another might be a noisy whirlwind and taking a calmer role in the story might let them see the value of such behaviour; a third might love adventure but never have the opportunity to take a lead, a child may be being bullied and you can give support and ideas through a story; and finally, a child may frequently be in bother for their behaviour and need to know that they are OK, that they are loved, that they can be who they are! These are just a few examples and I'm sure you can think of many more.

Over to you:

- What situation would you like to put the heroine/hero in? Write down a few examples.

- Do you want it to be familiar?

- Do you want it to be safe?

- Or a bit scary?

- Or magical?

- Or something completely different?

- Will your audience be able to understand and relate to it?

Nursery workers, teachers and others working with a group

- Do you want to link the situation to specific learning goals?

- Can you incorporate simple arithmetic for them to solve as part of the story? Or a language skill, or a route from home to the place of the story or similar curriculum demands? Do you need to do this – will it add to or distract from the basic story?

3) Story Development:

One thing to bear in mind when you are thinking of story development is that you need a **plot**. Basically, as mentioned earlier, all plots work to this formula – a **heroine or hero** is in a fairly normal **situation, someone else** enters the story and/or then **something happens** which **changes** everything and is **a problem or difficulty – the hero(ine) acts** to stop the person or save the situation, **all OK, the end!** Think about it and you're ready to begin.

Three-item, 30-second Stories

This first type of story is one of the simplest for telling to young children, especially when they are trying to get 'just one more story' out of you before settling down to sleep, or just before you leave.

Simply put, you ask the child to name **three random things**. Your task is to make up a story lasting approximately 30 seconds, which links all three things together. The child will be very impressed by this if you can achieve it. The time limit of 30 seconds does make it easier for you, as it limits the possibilities for deep plot development, but it doesn't have to be exact. Most children of that age won't be timing you, and it is a kind of bargain you are making with them – they will get a story, with subjects they choose – but only the shortest possible one!

Later, as they get used to the idea, you will find children attempt to make up their own stories on this basis. This is such a fun experience as both 'off the wall' and very well thought out stories appear. If your youngster can't quite manage it and is frustrated, do think of ways of helping them achieve it – maybe offering a prompt which has leads to an obvious conclusion to you but which will result in a very satisfactory story for them to tell you, and which they'll be so proud of.

Beware of other adults setting traps for you though – my youngest son joined in and enjoyed suggesting some really difficult subjects which did take quite a bit of thinking about before I could tell the tale! Just imagine...an elephant called Joshua, a donkey called Freydo and a birthday surprise! I hope that, like me, you'll refuse to be beaten! In our case, these characters are now regular favourites and have many strange adventures, shopping, going on holiday and so on.

Here is the first story which my three year old grandson chose the subjects for:

The Race, the Frog and the Chocolate

Thomas and Fini were racing on their bikes down the path near Nana's house and Suzi and Wanda were racing along beside them when...

very strangely...

a large turquoise frog jumped on the back of Thomas's bike and put his hands over Thomas's eyes.

Fortunately, frogs have long, spread-out fingers so Thomas could still see where he was going.

He called out to Fini to help him.

She reached into her backpack where she kept all her magic things and pulled out a piece of chocolate.

She threw it to the frog who ate it all up and became a little, ordinary, green frog again.

They took him to the pond and let him go, then they had a lovely picnic and raced back home.

(126 words)

~~~~~~~~~~

When the children are a little older, the same trick/technique can be used for longer stories as the following story shows:

The Ladder, the Vase and the Hat

Nana was out for a walk in the woods with Thomas and Finnja. It was a cold, icy and windy day, and suddenly Nana's hat was blown off her head and flew up into the air.

Thomas and Fini started running after it, but it flew higher and higher and then got stuck on a rock ledge high up above them. Thomas noticed a tree branch which was V-shaped lying on the ground, with some strong branches sticking out across it. He asked Fini to help him stick it into the ground.

As if by magic, it turned into a ladder, and Thomas began to climb up it whilst Finnja held the ladder steady just to make sure it was safe. Thomas began to reach for the hat but it was just inside a little cave and it seemed to be stuck.

"Why is it stuck?" he wondered. Well, as he lifted it, he realised that it had blown right over a little shiny vase on the ledge and was covering it up.

What a surprise! *It would be a nice present for Nana*, he thought. He passed the vase down the ladder, still inside the hat, for Fini to look after. When he got down and went to look at it, he realised it was made of ice and was starting to melt.

Nana looked at it and she loved it so she used her magic to turn it into a real glass vase until they got home, where she popped it straight into the freezer. Of course, it turned straight back into ice: a lovely shiny ice vase! Then Fini had a great idea; she filled it with chocolate and strawberry ice-cream and they all sat down and ate it for their tea.

(296 words)

~~~~~~~~~~

'Of course, it turned back into ice'. There is no 'of course' about this, no logic…it is magic! So, for the story to work, it depends on your belief in it – if you believe it then why shouldn't the children? If you are stuck, ask them what they think might have happened next. You can use their idea or you can say 'Good idea! But what actually happened was …!' If you have to do that, at least you have given yourself a two-minute breathing space in which to work the next bit out.

~~~~~~~~~~~

Over to you:

So, a little task for you now, please get yourself a timer of some sort and think about how you could include three of the following into a 30-second story.

<div align="center">

A dog   A child   A sock

A bear   A banana   A train

A skipping rope   Something else   A swing

</div>

- Give yourself no more than two minutes to try to think of it though – after all, if it were a spontaneous request from your children you would need to respond fairly quickly.

- After you've chosen the three objects, you can write down the story or just your basic ideas if you prefer. It is likely to be only 200 to 300 words long (the bit you've just read is just over 100 words). Don't worry about editing it in any way. Then, start the timer and set it for just 45 seconds to a minute, and tell your story out loud, even if there is no-one else there. Reading it out loud will make it feel more like the real thing! I've suggested the slightly longer time because your first 30-second story will probably take a bit longer (they all might be, but as long as they are 'short and sweet' does it really matter?).

- Alternatively, you can just make it up as you go along – i.e. as you are saying it out loud – imagine your audience are there if you don't have one at the moment. But please do use the timer. It will give you a real feel for the story. Read the two stories above out loud first, with the timer if you want to practise.

- After you've done this think about the story again. If you like it, write it down to keep in your writer's notebook (You have got one, haven't you!).

- If you don't like it, it is still worth writing it down and then you can try to work out why you don't. How could it work better? What do you need to change or what is missing?

Now, if you are brave, tell it to your children and ask them for three more items – and away you go!

Nursery workers, teachers and others working with a group

You may need to direct the story more, particularly in a large group:

- Think out your first example in advance;

- Ask the group to provide only two items, the third being your choice;

- Divide the group into smaller groups and ask each to come up with one character and/or situation. Work on a story together based on their ideas, to produce several stories from the group;

- Take sex/gender into account when doing the task – can stereotypes be broken or altered?

Good luck, enjoy it!

Please note that you will find it useful to write down all your stories once they have been told as you'll have a record of them. You may want to tell them to other children, you may want to alter some of it so that is more satisfactory, or you may want to enter it into a competition or send it off to a magazine for publishing. Later in your storytelling career, you may want to look at your own development since you first started and identify your strong points and those you need to work on.

Two-minute Adventure Stories

Once you become a successful storyteller with the children, and as they get older, you will find you need slightly longer stories. Here's a two-minute one.

Fini's adventure: Dancing, spinning with fairies

It was a lovely sunny day and Fini's brother, Thomas, had gone to play with his friend, so Fini was all on her own. She'd helped Mama for a bit, but now Mama was working and Opa (her German grandad) was there to look after her.

She picked up her little bag, with the magic wooden cat, Wanda, in it. She went into the garden and through the fence to a woody area. As

16

usual, she was singing to herself and then she started dancing. She was spinning round and round when suddenly she heard a lovely tune being played, but it was very quiet as if it was far away.

She wondered where it was coming from and started to look around and walked towards the big tree in the garden, but no, everything there was quiet. Then she turned round and went towards the lavender bush. To her surprise she heard a cross little voice say, "Why have you stopped dancing?" She jumped back and then looked around, but she couldn't see anyone. She knelt down and then started lifting up the leaves on the bush.

This time the voice was even crosser when it said, "Don't do that! You'll knock all my washing off the line!"

Fini stared and she saw a tiny little man with a blue hat and a yellow jacket. He was waving his stick at her. "Oh I am sorry," said Fini. "I didn't know you were there."

"No, that's the trouble with you humans," grumbled the fairy man. "You never notice anything!"

Fini said, "That's not fair! I notice lots of things and I've got a magic cat called Wanda!" She was going to lift Wanda out of the bag to show him, but then suddenly remembered that she wanted to ask the fairy man a question. "What is your name?" she asked. "And where is all that lovely music coming from?"

"Well, I don't know why you want to know, but my name is Mr. Nobodyman, and the music is the Fairy band. They are sitting just over there," he said as he pointed, "but I think you've broken the big bass drum!"

"Yes, she did," said a little mouse with a straw hat on. "I can't play it anymore." She looked so sad.

"Oh no! Sorry!" said Fini. "Can it be mended?" She picked up the little pieces and said, "I'll just ask Opa," and dashed back to the house.

Her grandfather looked at the drum and said, "Well I think I can mend it, but it won't sound quite the same anymore! Why don't I make a new one?" He looked in the kitchen cupboard and got out a little spice jar that was nearly empty. He washed it out, got the drum skin that had been on the fairy drum and carefully fastened it on with some thread. He tapped on it with his fingers and it made a little *ratatat*. "There you are," he said, "now you can go out and play with your dolls again." But Fini wasn't playing with her dolls, was she?

She rushed back to the lavender bush and called out, "Hello, Mr. Nobodyman, I'm back!" She put down the new drum and immediately the tiny mouse rushed up and grabbed it. She was just trying it out when Wanda the magic cat fell out of Fini's bag and turned into a real cat, as she always does.

The poor little mouse was very frightened but Wanda said to it, "It's all right. Why don't you and the others all climb up onto my back and you can play your tunes there?" Fini promised it was OK, so the mouse, lots of other tiny animals and people all with whistles and violins, a trumpet, a flute and a double bass, climbed onto Wanda's back whilst she lay down on the grass. Fini helped Mr. Nobodyman lift his grand piano on as well and and they all started playing.

Fini started dancing and and spinning round to the music and a few of the fairies danced and spun too as they played. Soon Mr. Nobodyman asked them to keep still because they were making him feel dizzy. Then, very gently, Wanda floated up in the air but no-one fell off.

After they'd had lots of fun, Fini could hear Opa calling, so she said, "We'll have to go now." The fairy creatures all climbed off Wanda's back and she jumped back into the bag and became a little wooden cat again.

"Bye!" called out the fairies.

"Bye!" said Fini, as she went off to see Opa and try the lovely biscuits he had just made.

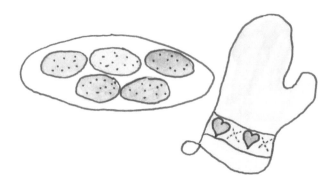

~~~~~~~~~

I nearly always seem to end my stories with something nice to eat...a nice reassuring ending!

~~~~~~~~~

The inspiration for this story came from two different things:

1) I wanted to write a story for my granddaughter, who as the younger child often gets overlooked if we're not careful.

2) I was on a train on my way to a meeting and a family with two children got on a couple of stops later. As the train pulled out, the boy called out to his sister, "Look, Mr. Nobodyman!" and they both looked enthusiastically out of the window at a figure in the distance and chattered away. I heard the name and realised that they had a story connected with him, and I thought it was such a good name that I could use it too. I wrote it down, and here you are!

Over to you:

Think of the stories you have just written/told, could you make one of them longer? Maybe expand on the problem to be solved or the actions of the main character(s)? Now is the time to try.

- So, using the same character(s), and using the timer again, try to develop your existing story into a two-minute version, or think of a new story for the same main character, or both!

- Share it with the child/children you want to tell tales to – what do they think of it? I'm sure they'll ask for another – try and think of one, just in case. They'll be happy to add a few suggestions for you to use (or ignore).

Nursery workers, teachers and others working with a group

Bear in mind that you need to keep the attention of a group young children for a longer period of time. You will have skills and experience to draw on so:

- Use your existing knowledge of the children to identify which children might be more easily distracted or might distract the others. How can you draw them in, in a way they will enjoy and which will avoid and distractions or diversions?

- How can you resolve any difficulties that might arise without spoiling the story for others?

Five-minute Adventure

As your child grows a bit older still, the stories will need to be a bit longer and more adventurous.

Thomas and Suzi's Tandem Adventure

Thomas was a bit older now, and he could do lots more things he liked without any grown-ups making all the choices for him. He still had Fini following in his shadow, of course, but she was so keen on dance and sports that often she was too busy to bother him at all.

He came out of his house and got on his mum's tandem, the one she'd used to take him or Fini shopping when they were first learning to ride a bike. She still used it now, of course, when Nana wanted to go with her, but the problem was Nana wouldn't always behave and often the tandem floated above the street as she shouted down to people she knew and made them jump!

Thomas wanted to use the tandem for a special reason, and he had put Suzi the wooden dog in his rucksack. He rode off to the middle of the woods where it was always thick and dark. He stopped the bike and let Suzi out of the rucksack. She turned into a live, magic, dog straight away. He called her and she jumped up on the back of the bike. He was determined she'd learn to ride it today.

At first she rode on the back and held on tight to him, but after they'd stopped for a picnic he told her that it was her turn to ride at the front – but she would have to pedal properly and to look where she was going! Thomas sat behind her and after a while, then, when Suzi seemed to be managing OK, he let go and leaned back with his hands in the air, just pedalling a little bit.

Unfortunately Suzi chose that moment to steer the bike down a steep narrow path towards the stream!

They wobbled and bumped as they sped along, over rocks, holes and tree roots. "Use the brakes, Suzi, use the brakes!" shouted Thomas, as he grabbed hold of her again. But poor old Suzi was scared; she didn't have a clue what to do, and *crash, splash*, they ended up in the stream, soaking wet and with the back wheel of the tandem looking a bit bent.

Suzi was so frightened by now that she jumped back into the rucksack and became a little wooden dog again – so Thomas knew he would have to sort the problem out all by himself! His ankle hurt a bit where he'd twisted it and he had a few little cuts and bruises, but he was OK. He was worried about getting home before it was dark though, and it was going to be difficult to get the tandem up the hill again on his own.

He reached into the rucksack, past the little wooden dog, to get out another sandwich to help him to think. As he did so, he felt Humphrey the clockwork spider in the bag. He'd never put him back on Nana's shelf after he'd borrowed him last time! "This is great," thought Thomas, "help is at hand!"

He lifted Humphrey out of the rucksack and immediately the spider came to life. Thomas explained the problem and Humphrey darted off amongst the trees to see how he could help.

He began to spin a thread rapidly and soon was able to turn it into a strong rope which he fastened round a tree. Thomas fastened the other end round the bent wheel and coaxed Suzi out of the bag again. They both pulled and pulled and soon the wheel was straightened up again, almost as good as new.

Then, whilst Thomas kept tight hold of one end of the rope, Humphrey untied the other end of it and went up to the top path, where he wrapped it round another tree and then threw his end back to Thomas. Thomas threaded it carefully through the tandem wheels so that the bike was fastened onto the rope. After that he checked that the rope was still wrapped round the bottom tree as well. Then he tied both ends together in a big loop to make something called a pulley...

~~~~~~~~~~~

A Pulley!

This is a hard idea to explain but gives an opportunity for an extra conversation.

*Question: "Do you understand what a pulley is?" If the **answer** is 'No' then try putting a rubber band round the child's fingers (or your finger and thumb if you are on Skype, for example) and letting the child (or you) move it round by pulling bit by bit. Explain how an object can be moved by a pulley if it is fastened to it and how doing this makes it easier to do. Even if the **answer** is 'Yes!' check discreetly just to make sure. In either case, encourage them to talk about it until it is clear they understand...THEN...back to the story! So...*

~~~~~~~~~~

...With Suzi holding up the middle of the tandem on her back and Humphrey making sure the rope didn't stick on the tree branches, Thomas was able to haul the bike back up the hill, because with the rope round the two trees it moved easily and pulled the bike with it.

Just then they could hear Fini singing in the distance and Suzi rushed to get her. Fini ran up and asked Thomas if he was all right. She gave Suzi and Humphrey a hug and asked them to get back in the bag. Then she untied the rope, which turned back into a silky spider's web on the top tree. She climbed on the front of the bike and, with Thomas and his rucksack on the back, they cycled safely home. For once, Thomas was really glad he had such a great sister!

~~~~~~~~~~

24

This story takes a longer time to tell because it is more complicated and because it is likely to start a conversation about how it all works, as many stories do. Take any opportunities like this that you can to discuss the story with the child or children; they may have to look things up, they may have their own solutions to the problem or incident you've described...and in any case, it's such a good opportunity to discover something new together.

Fini is given a secondary role on this occasion as the story was aimed at her older brother having an adventure on his own. Unfortunately, it is a little gender-stereotypical, with the male getting into trouble and the girl, supportively 'rescuing' him. However, I would argue that, as with Helen and Bobby, the roles would work equally well if reversed or could work with two same-sex children. Of course, you may need to include more than two children and will have to think out their roles by taking into account their gender, age, experience, relationship and character, as well as recognising which child the story is initially targeted at. The only example with several children that I have given you is 'Alfie's Golden Hour', which was designed 'to order' for his parents, and so favoured Alfie (at school) as its hero.

Over to you:

This story is for a slightly older child; it includes a problem for him to solve which is quite complicated and takes a little bit of thinking about before you (and so the character) can come to a solution – which then becomes obvious if you tell it again – 'Of course this is what would happen, why was I worried about it?'

- Review the stories you have invented and told already – why did they work?

- How could they work even better?

- Is there one thing in all of them that made you able to tell them and feel confident that you could work out an ending for them?

- Have you found your style, your 'theme' that usually runs through them yet? Mine is magic, yours could be too, or it may be animals, cars, dolls, the fact that you work at a school, or that you enjoy going swimming, for example. Try to identify it if it has arrived already make a note of it and try to tell a longer story using your theme to help.

- If you feel that it hasn't arrived yet, or you haven't got one particular theme, then go back to the stories you have already told and try to retell them with a different ending, or choose three new objects and tell a new longer story. Note how it feels different to you and which of the stories and styles you prefer at the moment. I promise you your audience will be pleased with the story and all the one-to-one attention they are getting from you.

Nursery workers, teachers and others working with a group

Don't expect it to be easy – you will have blank periods, everyone does, but DO expect that practice of any kind will make it easier and easier for you to do. And relax and enjoy yourself!

4) A Naughty Story

"A NAUGHTY STORY! Why a naughty story?" you say in horror!

Well, what better title to attract children of a certain age?

Children need to know that:

    a)   It **IS** ok to be naughty sometimes.

    b)   Other children are also naughty.

    c)   Not all naughtiness is intended.

    d)   Naughtiness can be put right.

and…

    e)   That grown-ups can be understanding.

A story with this theme can both amuse and reassure a child, and remind adults that a stern reaction is not always the most appropriate. This is the first one I wrote and it certainly amused my two.

A Naughty Story

Thomas didn't really mean to be naughty; he just saw what Fini was doing and thought it was funny. It had been raining overnight so there were lots of puddles on the garden path even though it was nice and sunny now. Fini was happily jumping in and out of puddles when she accidentally splashed Suzi the magic dog and the dog barked in surprise and shook herself over Fini, who just stamped her foot and splashed again.

Thomas ran towards them and joined in. This time he splashed Fini and Suzi at the same time. Suzi flew up in the air and shook herself over the top of the children and soon all of their clothes were muddy. So they ran round and round the garden, splashing, laughing, splashing and laughing.

Then Thomas had his idea. He decided to play a trick on Nana. He filled a bowl of water from the garden tap and then tied a big loop of rope round it. He climbed up the big tree and fastened the bowl onto a strong branch. He left one big bit of rope hanging down the tree for Nana to reach.

Then he asked Fini to get her from the house. When Nana came out she called, "What is the matter, Thomas? I'm busy baking some biscuits for teatime."

Thomas said, "Sorry, Nana, but I've got a trick to show you." Then he called out, "Just pull on the rope, Nana." Nana walked towards the tree and Thomas looked down at her. He was giggling away to himself, thinking how funny it would be when the water tipped on Nana.

But when he saw her he knew he had to stop her as she was wearing her best pinny and some baking gloves. He didn't want her to get those wet – he hadn't thought out his trick properly! He called out, "No, Nana!" and leant forward to hold the bowl to stop it from tipping.

But it was too late and Nana pulled the rope anyway. As the water began to pour out of the bowl, Thomas began to fall off the branch.

Nana worked her magic quickly. She turned the drops of water into flower petals and then she made the rope wrap itself round Thomas's ankle. Suddenly he was hanging upside down in the tree!

Fini and Nana started laughing and Suzi barked excitedly as she floated up to Thomas and licked his upside-down face. "Sorry, Nana!" said Thomas, and Nana lowered him safely down to the ground.

"You silly boy, Thomas," she said. "When I was baking I could see what you were doing out of the kitchen window – I'm glad you changed your mind about splashing me. Now let's all go inside, see if the biscuits are ready yet."

~~~~~~~~~~

It's quite hard to think of a 'naughty story' and it is probably best to work it out in advance...or you may find yourself tied up in knots! You may remember something naughty you did as a child that you can build into a story. So plan for the next time you will speak to/see the child or save it for after that real-life 'naughty' occasion. Don't offer it as a reward but as a discussion point or example to learn from. These kinds of stories are probably only suitable for six-year-olds and younger, as you can't make the story too serious without serious consequences of course, and after all, you are describing mischief not wrongdoing.

Over to you:

- Think who is going to make mischief/play the trick, girl, boy, animal...etc.

- Think who they will do it to – is it a parent, sibling, friend, other grown-up?

- Think how that character might react – you need a sympathetic character who will tolerate the action (as above). Or maybe a character who will be a little upset, so that the mischief maker has to put things right afterwards.

- Decide on what the action is to be. Make sure it is something fairly straightforward and easy enough for the listeners to picture and enjoy – anticipating the incident; but also...

- Make sure it is easy to put right, for example, if a child undoes a knot holding a toy boat steady and it starts to float away, make sure there is a way of recovering the naughty act easily.

- Finish with a smile, a warm ending – don't just end with little brother sulking and upset, or Mum very cross. The listeners won't find it satisfactory, they may find it worrying...and after all 'Everyone loves a happy ending'.

Nursery workers, teachers and others working with a group

- Is there a child in the group who demands attention, or becomes a nuisance to the class on occasions? Can they be helped by a story like this?

- Can the group as a whole learn anything from such a story through discussion/question and answers?

5) Stories that tackle a problem or deal with a new experience

Sometimes there are problems which young children have to face, like being isolated and over-shy with other people, being scared of dogs, or nervous about starting at new school. They may be aware of this but not able to tell anyone their concerns or it may be that they are upset but not sure why. Remember how you, as an adult, sometimes feel when faced with a new or challenging situation.

As adults we have to help the child deal with this in what we think is the most appropriate way for that child; that is, our choice of response, though equally sympathetic, will be different for each child dependent on what we see as their personality traits and what will make the issues easiest for them to understand and deal with.

Storytelling should be seen as an extra tool to help children begin to consider and resolve such problems for themselves. After all, that, in fact, is what stories are almost always about: having new experiences, meeting different people, resolving or facing difficulties, most of them ending with a positive result. So why not use them in this way to make things easier for our children?

This first one could be used to introduce a child to the idea of going to playgroup, 'kindergarten' or nursery school, which can be a bit of an awe-inspiring idea. The idea is that it can be told quickly and easily, just introduces the idea of going somewhere new, and ends with the child being reassured – but what it also does is offer an opportunity for questions to be asked and answered and anxieties uncovered and dealt with. There are lots of books available that aim to help children understand and accept changes in their lives; these are available through library services, in good booksellers and on the internet of course, but producing a personal story using characters the child is used to has a lot to offer. Here is one that just introduces the idea of going to nursery (kindergarten) for the first time.

"What's that?"

When Fini was quite little she went on her first adventure with Nana. Nana put Suzi and Wanda, the little magic wooden animals, in Fini's bag, she got hold of Fini's hand and off they all flew, up into the sky above the town.

"What's that?" said Fini as they floated up in the sky.

"Well, Fini," said Nana, "it's my house. Can you see the washing blowing in the breeze?"

"Yes," said Fini.

"What's that?" said Fini.

Nana said, "Well, Fini, that's Opa's greenhouse. Can you see him on the tractor in the field?" Opa looked up and waved to Fini and she waved back.

"What's that?" said Fini as she pointed ahead of her.

"Well Fini, it's a railway station - can you see the train? It looks small to us, but Papa is inside that train, going to work."

And, as Fini looked down, she saw Papa waving at her out of the window. She waved back and shouted, "Papa!"

They flew a little bit further and Fini said, "What's that?"

"Well, Fini," said Nana, "that is where Thomas goes to school. Can you see him with his red hat on? He's playing football before school starts."

"Yes," said Fini. "Thomas, Thomas, Thomas!" she called. Thomas and his friends stopped playing football and they all waved at Fini and ran along the ground right underneath them. Fini giggled.

"Nana, what's that?" asked Fini, pointing down to a street.

"That's where Mama works," said Nana. "Can you see her going into the shop?"

"Yes," said Fini (and Suzi and Wanda who had poked their heads out of the bag). "Hello, Mama!" shouted Fini.

"Why, hello, Finnja," called Mama and blew her a big kiss.

"What's that?" asked Suzi and Wanda, looking down at a big old house.

"Why, that's my new kindergarten," said Fini. "I'm going there today, but I don't know anyone. I haven't got any friends." She sounded a bit excited and a bit sad at the same time.

"You'll enjoy it," said Nana, "and soon you'll have lots of new friends."

Nana and Fini landed outside kindergarten and Suzi and Wanda said, "Can we come too? We can be your friends."

"Can they, Nana, please?" asked Fini.

"Yes," said Nana, "but only if they promise to stay in Fini's bag and not do any magic or any mischief all day."

"We promise," they said and turned back into little wooden animals at once.

"Hello, Finnja," said the teacher. "What's that?" she asked as she took Fini into her room.

"Oh, it's just my bag with my magic animals in it," said Fini as she turned, ran back to Nana and gave her a big hug, then ran back to the teacher. The teacher just smiled because she didn't really believe her. "Bye, Nana!" called Fini.

"What's that?" said Nana who hadn't heard her properly – but it was too late. Fini was already in the room playing with all her new friends, who were busy looking in her bag at Suzi and Wanda and saying, "What's that?"

~~~~~~~~~~~

This story shows the child as curious; everything she observes is a positive experience. So logically, when she gets to kindergarten it is positive too, something she likes. And there is even a little 'child joke' at the end, where Nana misses what is going on!

Over to you:

- Is there a situation that you as a child, or a child you know, have faced which might have been easier if you/they had understood what was happening beforehand? If so, try to make up a story to help, using that experience and thinking of it in a positive way.

- If not, think about one of the following and try to write a story to help a child in this situation:

    - A visit to the hospital

    - A very long journey

    - Being lost

Nursery workers, teachers and others working with a group

- How can you turn this story around to develop a welcome story for a new child?

A story for an angry child

Young children can sometimes be rude, angry or upset and not really know how to deal with it without losing face. They may well be feeling powerless to control what is happening to them, usually because they don't know how to explain what is bothering them, or feel that no-one ever listens to them or gives them a choice. Sometimes they may be jealous of a brother or sister, or even a parent who seems, unjustly, to be getting more favourable attention from the person who is the most significant to them at that moment, whether it is Mum, Dad, a grandparent or another person. They may not have experienced these kinds of feelings before or may have been scared of showing them because these emotions feel so powerful and overwhelming – out of control!

I was thinking about this and felt that a story describing the feeling in a child (under five years, I guess) might be useful to help the child realise that other people have similar feelings and also that it is possible to learn to control them and still have some control over what is happening to them too. It certainly won't offer an instant solution, but might be considered as one tool along the way which might help the child. I've called it 'The day Millie swallowed a volcano', but the names and gender of the characters can easily be changed to more appropriate ones by the storyteller, or it can be used as a model to suggest more fitting situations and issues in your own story.

See what you think!

The day Millie swallowed a volcano!

Uncle Dave was visiting Millie, her big brother, Jack, and little sister, Leah, one day, when he found out a very important secret about Millie. He had taken them to the park and had just explained that they were going down to the lake first, to feed the ducks, and that after that they would go to the playground, so they could all have a ride on the swings.

Leah and Jack seemed very happy, but, suddenly, Millie exploded!

Everyone was very surprised and Leah started to cry a bit.

Millie began with a very grumpy face, and then she shouted, "No!" at them all and stopped holding hands. Still shouting, she ran towards the swings and tried to climb on by all by herself.

Uncle Dave saw what she was doing and was worried that she might hurt herself. He called out to her, "Millie, stop! Wait for me!" and then he shouted, "Please be careful...look out for the swing!" as he ran towards her with the others.

You see, Millie couldn't climb on the swing by herself because it was a bit too high, so she had started to push it and it was wobbling about a lot and he was scared it was going to hit her.

Quickly, he popped Leah down on the playground floor and gave Jack the bag of duck food, and said, "Stay there, please!" and rushed to help Millie before she got hurt.

He dived forward and managed to grab her. He swung her round out of the way before the swing hit her. Then he put her back on the ground near the others.

He said to her, "Millie? I am glad you are OK. I am sorry I shouted, but I was worried in case the swing bumped into you and hurt you, you shouldn't have run off like that." Millie looked sad and started to cry. But Uncle Dave had had an idea. "I think you must have swallowed a volcano, Millie! Let me look down your throat."

Millie looked puzzled but she opened her mouth wide and let Uncle Dave have a look. "Yes," he said, "it's nearly gone now, but you did, you swallowed a volcano and it made you explode. It's not very nice is it, exploding? But I think we can get rid of the volcano if you'll let me help."

Millie wasn't very sure about any of this. She'd never heard of anyone swallowing a volcano before, and she didn't know whether to be frightened or excited.

Jack was very excited and started to sing, "Millie's swallowed a volcano, Millie's swallowed a volcano!" whilst he jumped up and down and clapped his hands. Leah joined in, running around and shouting, "Kano, Kano!" Millie thought this was quite funny so she ran over to them and joined in.

After a minute, Uncle Dave shouted, "One, two, three – Stop!" with a big grin on his face. Millie felt much happier now. "Let's have a look down that throat again, Millie!" Millie looked round proudly and opened her mouth wide, Uncle Dave had a quick look and said, "Yes! It's all gone now, Millie. Let's go and feed the ducks!"

As they set off down the path to the lake, Millie and Jack started asking questions whilst Leah kept singing 'Ducks' then 'Kano' over and over again.

"How do you swallow a volcano?"

"Does it hurt, Millie?"

"How did you know, Uncle Dave?"

"Has it gone forever?"

Uncle Dave swung hands with the children and talked as they walked along. He explained that anyone can swallow a volcano sometimes, because really it just means that they are feeling a little bit naughty or upset and also it might mean that they didn't want to do what they had been told to do.

But if that did happen, then they could choose to be more angry – so that the volcano starts to bubble up inside them, and then they would explode with crossness and shouting and feeling more upset; or they could choose to think about it as soon as the volcano started rumbling and put it out at once. They could do that by taking notice of what they had been told or asked, and if they didn't like it, they could ask nicely if they could change what they had to do, or what was going to happen, and give a good reason. Then the grown-up should listen to what they say and give them a fair answer. Millie liked that!

"Can it happen to grown-ups as well, Uncle Dave?" she asked.

"Yes, Millie, I'm afraid it can, but most grown-ups have learnt that it feels a lot nicer not to explode like that."

By this time they had arrived at the lake, and Jack gave everyone some bread out of the bag to throw for the ducks. Uncle Dave held Leah's hand and reminded them all not to go too near the edge. All the ducks came paddling across very fast and soon the bread was gone. Uncle Dave said, "Why don't we go to the swings now and then we can have an ice-cream on the way home?"

"No!" shouted Millie but this time she was laughing...and so that is just what they did!

Note that the adult does not 'give in' and let the child play on the swings straight away but goes back to the agreed original idea as soon as he has calmed the situation down.

Over to you:

- You may have ended the story differently; ask yourself why and then try to write down two or three sentences of how your story would end.

- Think to yourself: Does it work as a story? What's good about it? Would it ease the fictional situation and reassure a listening child that losing their temper may not be the end of the world?

- If you think it wouldn't work, that's OK too. Ask the same questions but look at why it doesn't work for you. Try to tell the story yourself – re-work *all* of it. Do it how you would like it to be, and write down why you think it works better.

- Write a completely different story looking at the same or similar problem.

Well done, if you've tried this exercise, which is quite hard. You really are well on your way to becoming a good storyteller!

Nursery workers, teachers and others working with a group

- How would you use this or a similar story to help your group understand the issue of temper and tantrums?

- Can you develop a similar story with the protagonist being one or more child(ren) in a group setting?

Note: For older children I would expect some help to have been offered to the child already and additional techniques to have been tried with greater or lesser success.

I would recommend the book, 'The Chimp Paradox' by Dr Steve Peters (2012, Ebury Publishing Co.) as it is an enjoyable, easily read book which allows the reader to consider why and how they respond to different life situations as they do, and how to deal successfully with the decisions they have to make. They can then apply this additional understanding to their children and their responses too. If my description sound a little heavy, well don't worry, it is just that I feel it is a book which would help many a parent or carer to understand what is going on for their young people, as well as themselves.

6) Story Games

I've included several games to play which I hope you will enjoy together. They are a good way of getting new ideas and also getting children to enjoy the idea of stories, reading, listening and sharing them with others. The points for you to try are pretty similar whether you are a parent or a teacher so the '**Over to you!**' sections are combined.

This is possibly the hardest chapter in the book for a new storyteller. You may never have come across these or similar games before and may feel a little overwhelmed by them. Don't worry – just read through them at this stage and see if you can make sense of them. Don't try to play them yet if you don't feel able to, you can come back to them later.

However, I can assure you they have all been played a number of times, they do work and are very enjoyable. But the age range is from about seven years upwards, as at an earlier age than this they can be a little confusing and frustrating. The older children will soon be playing them better than you though, once they have had a couple of goes – and will have a very clear understanding of the rules, which they'll keep you to!

The Backwards Story

The aim of these kinds of stories is for the end of the story to be given to the players and then anyone playing the game has to get back to the first line of the story by making up one line of the story in turn. They should make sure it fits with the end line but makes sense to the story as a whole (see example below). The grown-ups can offer prompts like 'Who is in the story? Where are they? Why are they there? What did it look/feel like?' to help them make it up.

These type of stories assume that the child(ren) is/are old enough to make imaginative leaps and also to follow the logic of a story (even backwards). You will be surprised at how young some children are when they reach this point and how much they enjoy doing it. It also assumes that the child is already aware of the basic characters you are using and any special abilities they have (e.g. the wooden cat and dog being able to turn into real animals when they come out of the rucksacks).

An example ending could be:

So, Thomas and Fini floated safely down from the top of the tree.

So what do you need to know to make it work? How did they come to be in the tree to start off with? That's the target you are working towards.

The easiest way to try to explain seems to be to expand the examples so you can see how they develop and then to discuss the best ways to make it work easily.

If we take the phrase '**So, Thomas and Fini floated safely down from the top of the tree**' and assume that there is one child and an adult involved, then the story might develop something like this:

Child (C): So, Thomas and Fini floated safely down from the top of the tree.

Adult (A): They both climbed onto the backs of the magic dog and cat.

C: Suzi the dog floated up to the top of the tree and Wanda the cat flew up there as fast as she could.

A: The little wooden dog and cat jumped out of the rucksacks, became alive, and ran towards the tree.

C: They called out to Suzi and Wanda to come and help them.

A: They suddenly realised they were stuck.

C: Thomas and Fini enjoyed climbing really high till they got to the top of the tree.

A: They decided to race each other up the biggest tree they could find.

C: They ran right to the middle of the woods.

A: They left Nana's house with the little wooden magic animals in their rucksacks.

C: Thomas and Fini decided to have an adventure.

A: The End – No...! It's the beginning!

~~~~~~~~~~~

If you are not sure that this makes sense, or that you quite follow it, try reading it again from the bottom upwards. Now you can see how it works!

It is difficult to do at first but imagine how amusing the child will find this, particularly when it is a successful story. Of course, an older child will enjoy diverting the story away from the logical start!

42

If the child is doing this for the first time it is often helpful for another older child or adult to discuss with them what might have happened with them 'secretly' for a moment, before the child gives their suggestion out loud. If more children are present the story can be unfolded as a 'round' in which each takes a turn (See Taking Turns game).

If there is just one child and one adult present, then the adult should help stimulate their thinking if necessary by telling a story they already know well, backwards, for example, Cinderella.

~~~~~~~~~~

Cinderella:

And they all lived happily ever after.

Cinderella married the prince.

The prince was delighted he had found her again.

She tried on the glass slipper and it fitted.

The ugly sisters both tried it on and were cross when it didn't fit.

The prince's servant took the glass slipper round all the ladies in the land to see if it fitted them.

She ran away from the ball and left one glass slipper behind, etc. etc.

~~~~~~~~~~

Over to you:

- You know how the story goes; just think what happened immediately before.

- Practise with a very well-known story like this and write it down from beginning to end.

- Then from end to beginning...

- Read it backwards to yourself until you have got used to the idea.

~~~~~~~~~~

Now, to go back to the previous example of Thomas and Fini's adventure, if the child wants to play the adult can offer prompts such as:

"How did they float down?"

"Who helped them?"

"How did they help them?"

"What else happened?"

"How did it start?"

And of course, the sentences the adult makes up are useful to lead the story back in a sensible direction and help the child think of its next idea.

~~~~~~~~~~

'Reach the End First' Story Game
(based on an idea from 'I'm sorry, I haven't a Clue' BBC Radio 4).

Here each child is given a different end line and has to try to move the story along to their own ending, whilst taking turns to give one sentence each.

This is really best suited for older children who won't take the answer given by the other children too seriously and enjoy anticipating how they can slip their ending into the story or stop the other(s) reaching theirs. It often works best with only two to four children taking turns to direct it, but then new endings and a new game can be played by other children who have been listening. Here's an example based on the following sentences:

The snowman ran back up the hill to the snow castle.

The snowman jumped off the wall into a big pile of snow and started to laugh.

To start:

The adult gives one finishing line to each child and explains that they have to take it in turns telling the story, one line at a time, and try to get it to finish with their own sentence. This is a competitive situation of course, but should be enjoyed by the children doing it – so the implied ground rule is that the children will not be mean to each other whilst playing the game and the adult needs to act as a fair referee.

44

Next, give the phrases to Child 1 and Child 2:

Child 1: The snowman ran back up the hill to the snow castle.

Child 2: The snowman jumped off the wall into a big pile of snow and started to laugh.

Let's assume that there are two children and an adult involved, then the stories might develop something like this, starting from the beginning:

Adult: One day it snowed very heavily,

C1: and...the snowman ran back up the hill to the snow castle.

C2: That's not fair!

~~~~~~~~~~

Oh dear, Child 1 has just used the sentence immediately! This is a matter of negotiation, and you will do it in the way that seems best for your situation.

Below are a couple of suggestions in case you are stuck!

Explain again it is meant to be a story which will have one of two possible endings but that no-one knows which yet.

Or, make sure the child starts the story next time and take the second sentence yourself to conclude the story – they will then realise why such brevity doesn't really work for anyone.

Give an explanation about how they are behaving, if necessary, or ask the second child to help you tell the story with their ending if they still aren't happy.

Think of two new sentences or just use the time to tell both stories yourself.

Let's begin again:

A: One day it snowed very heavily.

C1: The children built a big snowman.

C2: That night the snowman came to life.

C1: The moon lit up all of the hill.

C2: The snowman saw a big wall covered in snow just below him.

(C2 hopes to finish next time)

C1: But then he saw a big snow castle at the top of the hill.

(C1 hopes to finish next time)

C2: He got excited and started to run towards the wall.

(C2 hopes to finish next time)

C1: Then he slipped and spun round and started running up the hill.

(C1 hopes to finish next time)

C2: But instead of going to the castle, the snowman ran to the wall. Then he jumped off the wall into a big pile of snow and started to laugh.

A: Child 2 (name) wins!

OR it could go the other way:

A: One day it snowed very heavily.

C1: The children built a big snowman.

C2: That night the snowman came to life.

C1: The moon lit up all of the hill.

C2: The snowman saw a big wall covered in snow just below him.

(C2 hopes to finish next time)

C1: But then he saw a big snow castle at the top of the hill.

(C1 hopes to finish next time)

C2: He got excited and started to run towards the wall.

(C2 hopes to finish next time)

C1: Then he slipped and spun round and started running up the hill.

(C1 hopes to finish next time)

C2: Then he wondered what was on the other side of the wall.

(C2 is trying to rescue his/her story)

C1: But he couldn't see, so the snowman ran back up the hill to the snow castle.

A: Child 1 (name) wins!

~~~~~~~~~~

As the children get used to this game, the punchlines can become more sophisticated and less similar to each other.

Here are a few other suggestions for the end sentences:

And so John sat down in the middle of the puddle and played with the paper boat.

or

Then John threw the paper boat in the air to see if it would fly.

~~~

Jane ate all the chocolate cake mixture and hid in the cupboard.

or

Mum put the chocolate cake mixture in the baking tin and put it in the oven.

Together Time

Remember, games/exercises like this are encouraging the child(ren) to think about how stories are composed and to develop a sense of logic. Why not try making up a joint story with them? It may be longer and more complicated than you expect as all their ideas spill out, or it may be very, very brief! It doesn't matter! And remember, they might also like to develop a story themselves and share it AFTER it is finished – what a nice treat for you!

Choose a good 'together' time to do it, where you won't be interrupted. Listen carefully, perhaps recording what is being said, and the resulting story will be fantastic (don't forget to tell them that it is!). Use toys and household items as props if it makes it easier for the child to explain; sometimes they can't visualise concepts that we introduce that we think are very easy. Sometimes, they can't find the right words to tell us something but can show us. There is a great storytelling tradition related to this, of course – the art of using puppets!

Over to you:

- Using the examples above as guidance, think of your own punchlines, characters and abilities and how you would tell a story from the punchline.

- Do it with another adult a couple of times if you like – then you are ready to start playing it for real with the children! The bonus with this is, of course, that you are also practising your storytelling skills.

- Invent a couple of sentences for your own game.

- When you choose your sentences, think how you would develop the story in case they are stuck for ideas.

- What age are the children playing (it affects their behaviour choices for their character and problem-solving abilities)?

- Why would the character be in that situation in the first place?

- What are the alternative choices to make your stories work?

Taking Turns Game

This game title is almost self-explanatory. Get the children to sit in a circle, including yourself in it. If there are only a couple of children you will have to take a bigger part in making the story work. Explain to the children that everyone is going to help tell a story and that they should listen carefully to what the person before them has said, and think what might happen next until they think that the story is finished. You can add additional rules if you think you need to, but with older children you may want to see if they'd like to add some too.

The adult needs to start the story and it may take a few goes before the whole group fully understands the game. To start – why not start with the traditional:

A: Once upon a time, there was a girl named Petra.

C1: She lived in a big old house with her mum, dad, grandad and a cat called Smokey.

C2: She had a best friend called Robert.

C3: But all her friends at school teased her and said he was her boyfriend.

C4: She didn't like that, she thought it was soppy to have a boyfriend – she was only nine.

A: One day at school her friends teased her too much, and Robert got cross and rushed off to play with his other friends.

C1: Petra ran home from school and...

Well you can imagine the rest – she told her grandad and he offered a good solution, or she fell and hurt herself because she was hurrying and Robert helped her, or she fell and hurt herself and her friends were all sorry, or Smokey got very cross and chased all her friends away!

It could go many different ways but the young people will enjoy building on the story and will recognise a good ending.

With younger children it might go more like this:

A: Once upon a time there was a girl named Petra.

C1: She lived in a big old house with her mum, dad, grandad and a cat called Smokey.

C2: Smokey used to like to sit on Petra's head or her shoulder.

C3: One day she was having her tea and Smokey jumped on her head and fell off.

C4: He fell onto her plate and started to eat her fish fingers!

C5: Grandad got cross and shouted at Smokey.

A: But Smokey was a magic cat and he just turned into a grasshopper and jumped into Grandad's pocket.

C1: It made Grandad jump and his false teeth fell out...

Or whatever other nonsense they think of. They will love being as outrageous as possible, so don't forget to be shocked or horrified (and make them laugh). It doesn't really matter if the story is a 'bit daft', after all it is only a story!

~~~~~~~~~~

The next idea expands the ideas above and is probably better for children over seven years old.

A Mystery Story Game

Give each child the setting and start of a story with a mystery already established, for example Katie's kitten has disappeared but no-one knows how or where, or Michael's coat is not on his hook at school but everyone else is wearing their own coat. Think of the bare bones of the story, supply them with the characters. The children each adopt one and take turns in developing the story as before. BUT they all tell the story from their own character's viewpoint whilst the adult monitors and referees, i.e. they assist to reach a satisfactory ending – not necessarily a happy one – but until it is reached no-one can know which way it will go as it twists and turns as it moves along.

Filling in the Gaps Game

This game requires prior planning and need some different coloured card to write words on, say blue for proper nouns, red for verbs, green for everything else.

Type out a standard story leaving gaps where the names, some verbs and objects should be.

Make copies of the same words and add other unrelated ones and print/write them out as small cards on the different coloured card.

Cut to size.

Place the cards, in separate colour piles, on the table and then one person begins to read the story, pausing every time there is a gap.

The listeners then take it in turns at picking a card and reading it out as part of the story, which the main reader then continues with until the next gap.

For example, a story might start:

One day *Sally* (or) *James* went for a ride on a *bus*. When s/he got to the *playground* s/he ran over to the *swing* and *jumped* onto it. S/he started *swinging* and went so high that s/he *shot off* and landed in a *tree* and so on.

So, the words *Sally* and *James*, *bus, playground, swing, jumped, swinging, shot off* and *tree* and others such as *Freddie, Dad, a kitten called Sam, a car called Sunny*, **plus** *the names of the children involved* are written on cards placed face down on the table in their colours with other cards like *fire, sweet, elephant, chair, mushroom, school, running, eating, fell down, ran away, slug, shop, cow* for the listeners to choose from. Some very silly results are to be expected!

Story Box Game

Add a variety of items (up to eight) to a shoe box.

Make more than one box with different objects if more than four children are playing.

The children take turns in picking one item each from the box then they must work together with the other children in their team to build a story around the objects chosen.

And then tell the story out loud.

This can be either co-operative group-work, or if there are several boxes in use, a competitive element could be introduced with the children voting for the best story (not just for their own) and/or the adult having the casting vote.

Consequences Story with Picture Stickers

Picture stickers are sold very cheaply these days and a couple of different sets will change the old-fashioned game of consequences into a good story game.

Each child has one sheet of stickers, or several small selections of stickers – people, transport, fairies, animals, houses, toys etc. – and a sheet of A4 paper.

They choose one sticker, place it at the top of the page and fold the paper over just enough to hide it.

The paper is then passed on to the next child who sticks on another sticker and folds in the same way.

This continues until the bottoms of the pages are reached (about five turns).

The next child opens up the sheet and tries to make a story out of the pictures; e.g. a pig, met an egg, they rode on a fairy, they met a spacemen and jumped on top of a car.

Alphabet Cards

You can use well shuffled alphabet picture cards in a similar way to make another story.

Limericks and Poems

Finally, have you thought of introducing the idea of limericks to them?

Limericks are nonsense verses with five lines. But those lines follow a special rhythm pattern and really need to be read out loud for full enjoyment. There are plenty of books with them in and once you understand the rhythm you should enjoy making them up yourself – children may not fully understand at first – so that's why the reading aloud is important. Then they hear and learn the pattern and can begin to think of it themselves.

It just needs practise really.

Example:

> There was a young Teddy named Bill,
>
> Whose voice was exceedingly shrill,
>
> He stood on a chair,
>
> Called up in the air,
>
> And made Mummy say, "What a thrill!"

Here's how it works:

Lines	Rhythm

1. There was a young Teddy named Bill,
   da DUM da da DUM da da DUM (3 Dums)

2. Whose voice was exceedingly shrill
   da DUM da da DUM da da DUM (3 Dums)

3. He stood on a chair
   da DUM da da DUM (2 Dums)

4. Called up in the air
   da DUM da da DUM (2 Dums)

5. And made Mummy say, "what a thrill!"
   da DUM da da DUM da da DUM (3 Dums)

You could also introduce them to poems, especially ones which tell stories, and encourage them to learn them and/or re-tell them just as stories. They should enjoy getting to know and understand what poems are all about by doing this.

7) Planning and Designer Stories

Planning:

Now you have some experience of telling stories I'd like you to think of the process in which you have been involved.

1. You had to think of a character.

2. Then you had to place them in a particular situation.

3. You introduced other characters and objects or issues.

4. You thought of a dialogue between the characters.

5. You then changed the situation and created a problem for the character to deal with.

6. You described the character taking the action.

7. You then wrote a satisfactory ending to finish the story.

What you did was plan the stories before you told them. This applies whether or not you wrote them down first or just told them straight off. This may sound strange but I know from my own experience that just telling a story directly to the child/children does involve doing all those things and that sometimes I've had to think extra hard and extra quickly to work out what could logically happen next, because quite often I don't know until the character does something and I have to get them out of the mess they are (or rather I am) in!

Now I would like you to look at a formal way of doing this by writing a designer story. Here is an example of how you might do it.

Designer Story:
Alfie's Golden Hour: A story dedicated to Alfie Underwood, 2013.

This story came about because a friend's daughter was raising money for a 'gap year' project overseas. With her parents she organised a 'Skills Auction', and I volunteered to write a story for a child, provided that the successful bidder would supply me with certain details about the child concerned.

I designed the following questionnaire to give me the clues to the child's character and when Alfie's parents won the bid, I was able to have a few words with them also. I was a little taken aback as my original idea had been to write a story for someone six years old or younger as I had never really written much for an older age group. Alfie was nine years old.

I worried about the task and decided the best way forward was to look at several of my favourite children's authors and see how they dealt with this age group. I didn't want the story to be too young, embarrassing, or to be violent. But I did want it to be fun!

In the end I decided that a story situated in school would fix the boundaries well for me and was able to use his love of his dog, love of art and hatred of maths and then draw on his close friendships with other named children to complete the picture. I then checked with my friend (a teacher at the school) that my two made-up teachers did not have real-life counterparts: i.e. there was no Mr. Watson or Mrs. Green at the school. The story was then shown to Alfie's parents and I was told it was one which he would enjoy and so my task was over! Mission accomplished.

I am including it here as I felt that the template might give useful pointers for anyone trying to produce stories for a known child for the first time. It is a daunting prospect but a simple mechanism like this will help.

So will an understanding of, and empathy with, children of the same age group. Can you remember your school days? What one piece of mischief has stayed with you? What was the best fun you had there? Would your child enjoy hearing you tell them about this or something similar? Yes! Well there you are then…you are on the way!

Template for Designer Stories

Story for (Full Name): _____

A Designer Story for a child 9 years old or younger

Please answer my questions if you can. For a story about a particular child to succeed I need to know as many of the following details as you are able to supply. This is <u>only</u> so that the story can become as 'real' as possible for the child. Thank you!

Gender and age of the child: _____

Child's first name: _____

Nickname if any: _____

Names and ages of any brothers, sisters and/or cousins:

_____

_____

Home town or city: _____

Names used for Parents, Grandparents, Teachers or other important adults:

_____

_____

Names and gender of close friends:

_____

_____

Favourite pets/animals:

_____

_____

Really interested in (hobbies etc.):

_____

_____

Does the child attend nursery or school etc.:

_____

Is there any subject the child dislikes or which should be avoided?

_____

Are there any special subjects the child loves/enjoys:

_____

_____

Alfie's Golden Hour

Alfie enjoyed Friday afternoons best at school. They always had a 'Golden Hour', which meant that all the subjects were set up in different classrooms and you could choose the ones you liked best and book to go into them for an hour and then swap to a second one if you wanted to. He always chose art and computers. Alfie loved art and he enjoyed learning about different ways you could paint and draw, and about famous artists and what they did. Then he'd go to the computer class, do some new exercises and puzzles, go on the school intranet and talk online to Jake, Alex and Joseph, even though they were usually sitting next to him in the classroom.

But today was going to be extra special, as the whole day was going to be a 'Golden Day', as the school was raising money for a children's charity. You could pay to go into any classroom for the whole morning or afternoon, or you could go round each class in turn as long as you paid at each door. Everyone except Mr. Watson, the new maths teacher, was charging £1 to go in. Mr. Watson was offering a bargain session for only 50p. Alfie thought it was because Mr. W was desperate for pupils to go into his room!

The school had also had another good idea. They had converted the school field into a 'Pets' Corner' and everyone could bring a pet into school for the others to see. So Alfie was taking his dog, Maisie, in with him, and he was sure, with all the tricks he had taught her, she could easily win the prize for most talented pet. There was going to be a show just before home time, and he was really looking forward to it.

When he got to school he went quickly down to the 'Pet Marquee', where the animals were being kept for the day. It was really the local scouts' large dining tent and was beginning to look a bit crowded already. He took Maisie behind the tent and quickly practised her favourite tricks with her. Jumping, waltzing on her back legs and counting. She was so good at counting that she could lift up each paw in turn when they needed wiping as Alfie said 'one', 'two', 'three', or 'four'. Then Alfie got her settled in the dog area and dashed off to the art room to spend some time drawing cartoons. Alex had gone to history, Joseph to science, and Jake had gone to see if he could take part in the sports heptathlon.

But Alfie had made himself a bit late by doing that extra practice with Maisie, and to his horror all the places in the art room had gone! What could he do now? He was really upset, as he had been looking forward to it so much. He dashed to the English group in the library but that was full too, then to the computer room but, as he had guessed, that was also full.

Downhearted, he made his way back to the Pets' Corner and started to draw pictures of all the animals in the sketchbook he always had with him. There were four dogs, five cats, a goldfish in a round bowl, six guinea pigs, a rabbit, a frog, three white mice, a corn snake and a parrot called Itsbi. There were also three lambs, a goat and two ducks, from the local farm. They were all in separate pens, of course, and Alfie noticed that each pen was a different shape. The dogs were in a smallish square pen, the cats in a large circular one but each in separate boxes; all the small animals and the goldfish were on tables in a triangular pen; even the snake was in there sleeping happily with a warm lamp shining down on its tank. Finally the lambs and the goat were in a wooden fenced-off oval shape, with the ducks in the middle in an old metal bath.

Mrs. Green, the teacher in charge, sat near the door of the tent, reading a book and coming over occasionally to look at what Alfie was doing. Alfie had an idea when he saw the shapes of the animal pens and began to draw cartoon animals inside each shape he could see. He asked Mrs. Green if he could let Maisie out, as she was looking so sad and was always so well behaved. Maisie lay down across Alfie's feet and he continued to draw.

That was when the trouble started! Alfie decided to move closer to the small animals so he could see them better, but Maisie had decided she needed to do some more practice of her tricks. She stood on her back legs and started spinning round, round and round, round and round, round and then...CRASH! She banged into the table with the snake tank on it.

Maisie was a bit frightened of the snake as it began to slither across the floor, towards the mice and the frog. Head and ears down, front paws forward and her back in a low arch, she began to make a whimpering, barky, growling noise and edged slowly closer to it.

Alfie decided to move her out of the way before he began the rescue. He grabbed her collar, tried to tell her it was all right, and led her towards the square pen. But the cats had been frightened and started yowling, the other dogs began to bark, the lambs baaed and began to jump around and then the goat leapt out of the pen, knocking over the table the goldfish bowl was on. Alfie did a splendid rugby-style dive and caught the bowl just before it crashed onto the ground.

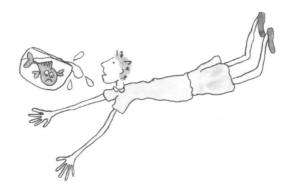

All the noise had attracted other people. Mrs. Green was trying to catch the snake with a cardboard box. Jake, Joseph and Alex appeared and started getting the mice, the frog and the guinea pigs out of the way, and then the snake turned its attention to the ducks. Other children appeared; some were screaming, some crying and some just laughing at what was happening. Alfie quickly handed the goldfish bowl to Eve, the tallest girl in his class, and went to try and help Mrs. Green. Itsbi the parrot didn't help by calling out, "It's behind you! It's behind you!" in a more and more frantic way.

Then someone shouted, "Be quiet, will you, please! What's going on here?"

It was Mr. Watson. He had left his class, as it was a bit quiet, and come out to see what the noise was. The children stood still, the dogs stood still, the cats lay back down, but the mice, the lambs, the goat, the guinea pigs, the ducks and the snake kept on moving, and of course Itsbi kept on squawking her cry: "It's behind you! It's behind you!"

"OK, let's get organised," Mr. Watson said as he moved to get the warm lamp and took the snake's tank over to where it was, near the ducks. He gently picked up the snake. "Come on, Sylvie, no need to be frightened," and he popped her back in the tank, put the cover over and, placing the snake in the circle, he replugged the lamp over it.

Then the remaining animals had to be rescued! Alfie ran after the goat, which was now out on the field munching happily; Maisie rounded up the lambs whilst Jake held the pen gate open for them. Joseph and Alex quickly checked that all the other animals were OK and Mrs. Green went off to get everyone a drink.

When Alfie came back with the goat, Mr. Watson and the others were all very pleased with themselves, until Alfie pointed out that half of the animals were in the wrong pens and that some of them were quite squashed up. He showed Mr. Watson his cartoon and the teacher did a headcount of animals, then looked at the tables and the pens. "We'll soon sort this out," he said. "OK, Alfie, which ones first?"

Alfie said he thought that the dogs should go in the big circular pen where they didn't need to be fastened up, because they all seemed to get on well. "Right, that's the first five in! What next?" said Mr. Watson happily; then Alfie and Alex quickly moved the small animals, except the snake, into the oval with the duck bath. "And now?" Mr. Watson asked, and Jake and Joseph moved the cats into the triangular pen. Finally the goats and lambs were put in the square pen, where there was a bale of hay for them to nibble.

That left just the snake, the goldfish and Itsbi to sort out. Mr. Watson moved Itsbi to the door of the tent, where she could chat to everyone as much as she liked. The goldfish bowl and table went next to Mrs. Green's seat, and the snake was put in quite a darkish corner with the heat lamp glowing away on it.

Alfie was just doing new sketches for the school newsletter when Mr. Watson came up and grinning said, "Applied mathematics, eh, Alfie?"

Alfie shuddered; he still didn't like maths but he'd love to get to know Sylvie the snake better and at least he could see some use for maths, helping to sort everything out.

"Applied art, sir!" he replied.

Oh and yes, Maisie did win the show...

...with Itsbi a close second, and Sylvie the snake coming third!

Over to you:

- Think of a child you would like a designer story written for (even if that child is you as a child).

- Fill in the form as much as possible from your existing knowledge of the child.

- Try to think of their character and what sort of adventure they would enjoy being part of (the hobbies, pets and so on will give you a few clues).

- Now, plan the outline of a designer story for them, review your plan and write the story in full, even if it is really short.

- Think of reading it as the child you thought of – would the child act like that? What would the child spot, if they read your story, which wasn't quite how they would act? Is the ending a satisfactory one for that child?

8) A story for a new baby and his or her parents

On a personal note again, we now have a new baby, Kian, in the family, and his parents had expectations already that Nana would write and tell him stories too. Here is his first story, and he has a second with his cousin, Finnja, in it too. A little early for him to understand yet...but still! If there is a new baby on the horizon for someone you know, writing a story about the child and its family, once the baby has arrived, would make a great, original gift.

Baby Kian builds a ladder

Extraordinary things always seemed to happen when Nana was around. Nana wasn't a witch; she just had a little bit of magic at the end of her fingertips, as most nanas do. Suzi and Wanda were her magic animals; they looked like a wooden cat and dog that sat on Nana's shelf, but she always took them with her in her big handbag, and sometimes some other toy animals too. When they were allowed out of the bag they became real animals who could do extra special things!

Today was a special day for Baby Kian; Nana had come to visit and brought some lovely balloons, three shaped like stars and one shaped like the moon. She got them out of her bag, rubbed some 'Spelling Cream' on them and they all flew up and floated in the middle of Baby Kian's bedroom.

Nana had let the little wooden cat, Wanda, out of her bag and she had become a real cat as usual, but poor old Suzi the dog wasn't allowed out as she chased balloons and accidentally popped them.

Kian loved the balloons and got very excited. He started stacking his building bricks into a ladder shape and began climbing up them to reach the balloons.

What Kian didn't quite understand yet was that ladders need to rest against something or they fall over. So after a moment the ladder began to wobble and bricks started to fall. Wanda gave a big *Meeeeooooow!* and flew up in the air to catch the baby before he fell.

As she did so she knocked over Nana's bag and Suzi fell out and turned into the magic dog. She was very excited when she saw what was happening. She kept taking bricks away from the bottom of the ladder and building it up again at the top, making it start to float around the room, whilst Wanda struggled to hold Kian by steadying him with his jumper in her mouth. What a strange sight! Kian loved it and clapped his hands.

Then Suzi had a good idea and floated over Wanda and Kian was lowered onto her back. Suzi started chasing the balloons and Kian grabbed hold of the string of one of them and floated around away from Suzi.

Nana came in to see what was happening and started laughing as Suzi popped a balloon and a beautiful star came out of the middle and floated up to the ceiling.

Kian squealed with delight and so Suzi popped two more. Then Wanda, who was frightened by the noise, got stuck on the ceiling too!

Kian clapped his hands again but forgot about the moon shaped balloon he was holding and it floated up as well. Nana caught Kian as he fell and Wanda pushed the balloon very gently with her paw and it came back down again. Kian tapped it and it went back up. They had lots of fun and Wanda forgot to be frightened and began to float back down to the floor. As she did she accidentally popped the last balloon and jumped right up to the ceiling again in fright. The little moon that came out of the balloon floated up as well and all the stars began to twinkle.

Nana lifted Kian up high for a closer look and asked Suzi to help Wanda down again. When they were both down on the floor, she put them back in her bag as little wooden animals, gave Kian a big hug, snuggled him and sang him to sleep.

Over to you:

*   Think of a special occasion that you might like to write a story for: a new baby, a special birthday, a wedding or engagement.

*   Think back about the person/people most involved in the occasion; what would they like to be reminded of, to keep as a souvenir of the event, to treasure in the future?

*   Make notes which will guide you (a bit like the designer story) – you can exaggerate or include ridiculous/humorous events – provided you know the person well enough (whether adult or child) to know they will enjoy it.

*   Write, edit and present your story.

9) Family Tales

I thought it was worth mentioning family tales, as there is a great deal of interest from children about past members of their family. They love to be told of the time Great Uncle John got stuck in a revolving door, or the time when Auntie Jane put too much baking powder in a cake and it rose high and then splashed all over the inside of the oven…or whatever the story was.

For my family, one story is of Great Grandad Wilf (my dad) as a young boy, secretly replacing the insides of some crème chocolates with mustard, replacing the chocolate he had cut from underneath and putting them back in the box. Then watching his father eat them, without any expression of surprise or concern, and Wilf *never knowing* whether he had noticed or not!

And who could fail to be riveted by the idea that my middle son, at the age of five or six, made up a song, "Trees are underneath the bridge, la, la, la la, la, la, la la," and sang it in the car – without pause, so it seemed – for almost an hour and a half on the way to a holiday in the Lake District? Lots of questions here, like: 'Why did he do that?', 'What did it sound like?' and so on. And then the children singing it themselves, and their uncle secretly grinning as he remembered.

Remember, these stories are all completely personal to your family, they may be remembered in different ways by different family members but they are passed on with enthusiasm as people smile and remember being told the story themselves or actually seeing the incident happen and being amused by it…and now I can't get that song out of my head as I've told the story to you!

Such tales will become part of the family history but also act as a little bit of cement in keeping the family unit together over many years. They provide a good talking point and will inspire other memories of different incidents.

Equally interesting for the family is to record all the names of people you can remember hearing about within the family, writing down anything you can remember, whose side of the family they were on, whose sister, brother, child parent they were, where they lived and anything about them that will bring them to life a bit. If any of the family later decides to research a family tree this information will be really helpful and those people in the past will remain in the family memory for a bit longer.

You could start one with the children with just the generations they are already aware of, and then add the generation prior to that. Include photos or let the children draw the people as they imagine they might have been. They will enjoy mapping it all out and understanding the logical order of their family and the story of their lives. Maybe they would like to make up stories about those they have learnt about!

Over to you:

- Just get rustling up those memories, souvenirs, photos and relevant dates and see what you can do with them.

Nursery workers, teachers and others working with a group

- Can you turn this into a group history project with children bringing objects and/or stories from home to help build it up?

10) Summary – Telling Tales

Many people may never have considered telling a story to children, or certainly not writing one down. Many will find the idea quite daunting.

Please don't let the idea worry you. Just relax and enjoy whatever you can offer. We all have ways of responding to children. Don't worry about getting it 'wrong'; there isn't a right way to do it other than getting the children's attention and keeping it by telling something that they can engage with. After all, even scary stories can be enjoyed to the full – just pitch your story at the right level for your audience.

It may be that you can just tell them about your own childhood experiences – this is invaluable to children – not only as the 'history' of your life, which they can learn from, but also as a way of understanding their own experiences. And what child doesn't enjoy hearing the mischief or adventures their parents, aunties or uncles, older brothers and sisters got up to at the same age? They will ask for these tales again and again. Or you may be good at making up little rhymes or limericks for them to enjoy. You can teach them nursery rhymes and make up additional things about those characters, and you can have a 'sing-along' as well!

Sitting on the bus or in the car with them you may notice buildings, places, people, animals which you can tell them more about.

The 'gift' of storytelling is really just a combination of different skills, listening to the child and using their language rather than an adult one. It is remembering what it felt like to be a child, and describing things from their perspective, and listening to and observing what's happening around you, and like all skills it can be developed and built upon.

If you can manage to write it down, all the better, as if they have enjoyed your stories, the children are likely to ask for them again. Also, in the long run, they will have a memento of their time with you. Or why not use a cassette recorder, an iPod, or your phone to record the stories? You may find it easier to just jot down a few words as prompts. Or you may have a talent for doing little sketches to go with the stories and/or act as reminders instead. In fact, if you find it easier to draw or take photos you could make a cartoon style/photo-journal story for them instead

Above all, just relax and enjoy your time with them! Do what seems to work for you; please don't worry about it if storytelling still doesn't seem right for you. Why not read other stories from the library to them, if you can't manage your own, and enjoy extending your positive relationship with them in this way instead? Why not join a local writers' group or help at a playgroup and practise your skills there before getting fully involved with telling your own tales?

So with delight I now say –

"Over to you!"

Over To You

Lightning Source UK Ltd.
Milton Keynes UK
UKIC01n0305290815
257759UK00003B/4

* 9 7 8 1 9 1 0 6 3 5 3 4 6 *